March 2006

Jerry —

It's your day — enjoy!

"Happy Birthday"

Regina

The Wit & Wisdom of

Bobby Jones

The Wit & Wisdom of

Bobby Jones

Edited by Sidney L. Matthew
Foreword by Bob Jones IV

CLOCK
TOWER
PRESS

Illustrations by Ed Lloyd
Foreword copyright © Robert T. Jones IV
Text and illustrations copyright © 2003 Sidney L. Matthew

Clock Tower Press, LLC
320 North Main Street
P.O. Box 310
Chelsea, MI 48118
www.clocktowerpress.com

Printed and bound in the United States
10 9 8 7 6 5 4 3 2 1

Library of Congress Cataloging-in-Publication Data
Jones, Bobby, 1902-1971
The wit & wisdom of Bobby Jones / edited by Sidney L. Matthew ;
foreword by Bob Jones IV ; [illustrations by Ed Lloyd].
p. cm.
ISBN 1-932202-09-9
1. Jones, Bobby, 1902-1971--Quotations. 2. Golf--Quotations, maxims,
etc. I. Title: Wit and wisdom of Bobby Jones. II. Matthew, Sidney L.
III. Title.
GV964.J6A3 2003
796.352'092--dc21   2003004726

To Charlie Yates, my hero and my friend.

A wise-cracking, happy-go-lucky protégé of Bobby Jones down in Atlanta whose high spirits were so infectious that he accomplished the unprecedented feat of standing on the steps of the Royal and Ancient Clubhouse at St. Andrews after the 1938 Walker Cup match and inducing the crowd to accompany him in *A Wee Doch and Doris...* "Lang may yer lum reek."

Foreword
By
Robert T. Jones IV, Psy.D.

On first glance, the idea of publishing an entire volume devoted to an athlete's humorous sayings and writings seems unusual, to say the least. Athletes are not generally noted for their ability to coin a phrase. One possible exception to this might be a compilation of the unusual phrases of Yogi Berra, such as, "When you come to a fork in the road, take it." However, nobody would complement Berra for his great contributions to literature. This is not to say that athletes are stupid people. Rather, we recognize that athletes have to devote enormous amounts of time and energy to reach a level of achievement in sport about which most people can only dream. That sort of devotion means that athletes usually don't develop other skills that would make them candidates for a book such as this one.

My grandfather, Bobby Jones, was a notable exception. Maybe only once in a century does an athlete come along that can scale the competitive heights that he scaled: Thirteen major championships in seven years and the Grand Slam in 1930, the event that *Golf Digest* called the single most important accomplishment of the 20th century. While Bub, my family's nickname for my grandfather, was competing in golf championships, he was also getting an education. He earned a bachelor's degree in mechanical engineering and a second bachelor's degree in English literature from Harvard. When he finally decided to become a lawyer, he attended Emory University in Atlanta. He passed the bar examination and was admitted to the Georgia Bar after only one semester of law school. I was privileged in 2002 to accept the Emory Law School's Distinguished Alumnus Award on his behalf. I believe it was the first time that they had given this honor to a man who never formally completed his law studies.

Words were always very important to my grandfather; hence, he treasured a good wit and the ability to express concepts and ideas. I have been told that he used to keep a copy of a five page letter in his desk. When a young lawyer would have him review a brief that Bub felt was too long, he would take the letter out of the drawer and have the young attorney read it aloud. The last line: "Please forgive me for writing such a long letter, as I did not have time to write a short one." Young lawyers usually got the point that good argument was not directly proportional to the number of words used.

I am hard-pressed to think of another athlete who was or is as literate as Bub was during his life time. When most players would retire to the bar after a round, Bub would soak in a bathtub, sipping a glass of scotch and reading Papini's *Life of Christ*. Not too many athletes would concern themselves with the writings of Shakespeare and Dante, but Bub would read them, as well as many other authors. As a result, Bub was not scared to turn a phrase and was as adept with the pen as he was in the spoken word.

Furman Bisher, the great sports writer from *The Atlanta Journal Constitution*, told the story about the time when he was hired by a national magazine to have Bub describe his play in championship golf. The by-line was to have read, "By Bobby Jones, as told to Furman Bisher." When he heard this, he declined, telling Bisher, "Good God, Furman, people will see that by-line and think that I can't write a simple sentence." Writing an English sentence was something that Bub did with remarkable skill. In his lifetime, he wrote a regular newspaper column and several books. He prided himself on his writing ability and that he did not have to rely, as did most athletes, on ghost writers. An example of his turn of phrase was in his famous description of the game of golf:

"Golf may be...a sophisticated game. At least, it is usually played with the outward appearance of great dignity. It is, nevertheless, a game of considerable passion, either of the explosive type, or that which burns inwardly and sears the soul."

Another centers on his description of golfers:

"On the golf course, a man may be the dogged victim of inexorable fate, be struck down by an appalling stroke of tragedy, become the hero of an unbelievable melodrama, or the clown in a side-splitting comedy—any of these within a few hours, and all without having to bury a corpse or repair a tangled personality."

Bub's verbal agility also emerged in family life and casual golf. Once, at Highlands Country Club in Highlands, North Carolina, he played a casual round of golf with my dad. Dad was not having a good day and his clubs spent almost as much time in the air as his golf ball. After watching this for a few holes, Bub turned to his caddie, Dugan Reese, and looking at my dad said, "You know, Dugan, sometimes it's not the arrow, it's the Indian."

Another episode involved an unusual foursome match at the Atlanta Athletic Club's East Lake course. In what had to be a moment of weakness, Bub decided that it would be a good family outing to have a foursome (alternate shot) match between Bub and my aunt Mary Ellen, versus my father and my grandmother. My grandmother was not a good golfer but she was reasonable. My aunt, however, had never played before. So on the first tee, Bub hit a magnificent tee shot and Mary Ellen dribbled a shot about four feet. It was probably her best shot of the day. Bub endured his youngest daughter's lack of skill better than most would, but finally he could take no more. As they stood on the tee of the sixth hole, a short par three almost totally surrounded by water, Mary Ellen stood on the tee and said, "What should I do here, Daddy?" Bub could no longer contain himself. He looked at his beloved daughter and through clenched teeth said, "For God's sake, just whiff it."

Another great wordsmith is Sidney Matthew, the man who has assembled this volume. Sid began researching my grandfather almost two decades ago and probably knows more about Bub than any living person. Through all the years I have known Sid, he has always combined a generous spirit with an intellectual curiosity that would have pleased my grandfather. To me, he has been a wonderful friend and I hope you will enjoy this volume.

Introduction

By
Sidney L. Matthew

The afterglow from centennial celebrations of Bobby Jones' birthday in March 2002 have prompted many to ask, "Why is it that Bobby Jones is still so popular even thirty years after his passing?"

The quick answer is that we have yet to see anyone quite like him. Jones was not just the greatest player of his era and perhaps of any era, but he was also the most intellectually gifted observer of golf and life. Jones suffered through the crucible of competition which unequivocally qualified him to write about all aspects of the sport. He was also a keen observer of the human condition. If you couple these gifts with his skillful ability to communicate his ideas on paper, one can readily appreciate why Jones' wit and wisdom are still valued today.

Decades after Bob Jones retired from the major championship circuit, which he dominated as ever did any player since, Jones chuckled when he read that a newcomer had "discovered" a startling new truth. When Bob read the latest revelation, he often saw something familiar. That which was pawned off as original was actually a recycled, theorem, or statement Jones himself had penned years earlier!

As a lawyer, Jones well knew his rights. But, he never rudely went after those who plagiarized his earlier works. He was too much of a gentleman for that. Instead, he chuckled quietly to himself and treated the lack of proper attribution as a back-handed compliment. Jones wrote about this in his book *Bobby Jones on Golf*:

Nothing in my continuing observations of the great players has caused me to alter my convictions and it does appear significant that even today I find coming back to me in spoken words, and from the printed page, phrases I wrote more than thirty years ago. I mention this not at all as a complaint because I am pleased to have confirmation of my views from the expert players and writers of today.

The enjoyment of Bobby Jones' wit and wisdom has not been dulled by the passage of time. In fact, the modern poet laureates of golf, including Herbert Warren Wind, Pat Ward-Thomas, Peter Doberiner, Charles Price, Bernard Darwin, Henry Longhurst, to name a few, have acknowledged Jones' literary contributions with acclamation. Has there been anyone on the horizon to replace him? How about anyone who might claim to be his equal? So far, there have been no candidates. That alone confirms that Jones' descriptions of the essence of golf are well worth consumption by those who love the game today. Surely Jones would crease a smile as we read these even now.

Instruction in Golf

I have never had any better advice in golf from tee to green than was contained in a telegram sent me by Stewart Maiden in 1919. It read: "Hit 'em hard. They'll land somewhere."

•

The first requisite of a truly sound swing is simplicity.

•

More short pitches are missed because of an abbreviated backswing than for any other reason.

•

No putt is short enough to be despised.

•

Probably the most common failing of the average golfer is to swing the club almost entirely with his arms and hands, omitting the use of any sort of a turn of his hips and body.

I have attempted to stress many times the importance of starting the backswing mainly with the left side in order to encourage a full extension of that arm.

•

The best exercise for golfers is golfing.

•

I think that most people have trouble with the less-than-full shots because they restrict the backswing too much.

•

I always try to emphasize the importance of an ample backswing. We see so many golfers who begin hitting before they reach the top of the swing. They go back fast and then they get in such a rush to hit the ball that they yank the club down before they fairly get it back. I never play well unless I swing back slowly and make certain of reaching the top before I start down.

Most failures from bunkers or rough results from topping and this is so because tension has upset the stroke.

•

The almost universal tendency is (for the ball) to creep more and more ahead until the player suddenly finds out that at address the ball is directly opposite his right foot when he would have sworn it was opposite his left.

•

I have found little value in the maxim "keep your eye on the ball" except on the putting green and in playing very short approaches. I always think of it as "staying down to the ball."

•

Hitting too soon is a fault of timing in itself. It results in the player reaching the ball with a large part of the power of the stroke already spent.

The most trying time of the year for the golfer is always the time when he comes out of hibernation and begins to try to tune his game back to a point where he can again enjoy it.

•

It doesn't help a great deal to have the soundest swing in the world if that swing is not trusted.

•

The knee-action of a golfer is so closely related to the motion of his hips that it becomes almost impossible to separate the two. It is even difficult to determine whether certain movements originate in the legs or elsewhere. In addressing the ball, I have always found it best to allow both knees to be slightly bent as an aid to relaxation, and in order to be able to respond readily to the first movements.

•

The third common tendency is to attempt to lift the ball instead of striking it firmly downward.

I have found that to turn both feet slightly outward obtains the best balance between the backward and forward turns of the body.

•

There is no hazard like the wind, for it affects every shot or every hole from the tee to the bottom the cup and what it fails to do to the ball in the air, it does with interest to the morale of the player.

•

The simplest view of the putting stroke is that it is in miniature just like any other stroke in the game.

•

It is not hard to prove that the besetting sin with the vast army of golfers is a failure to hit through with the left arm and hand, attended by a tendency to permit the right to overpower the left.

I think that in putting, as in making every other golf shot, the player ought to forget about his head. Think with it, but not of it.

•

The danger of "looking up" apparently becomes greater as the length of the shot becomes less. Rarely do we see an indication of "looking up" when the player is driving or playing an iron shot. Sometimes the head comes up and the shot is spoiled, but I think this is caused more by a resistance elsewhere in the stroke forcing the head away than by failing to look at the ball. In other words, the head lifting itself results from a mechanical fault, and does not itself start the trouble.

•

In the second place there is a feeling of better and easier balance. There is less tendency to hit with the body, a fault that has driven several million golfers into the borderland of melancholy depression, year after year.

Never up never in—of course we never know but the ball which is on line and stops short would have holed out. But we do know the ball that ran past did not hole out.

•

The only one who has a chance to achieve a rhythmic, well-timed stroke is the man who in spite of all else yet "swings his club head."

•

The putting stroke is the simplest of all because it is the shortest, and once a person develops a fairly good sense of what it is all about and once he has developed a rhythmical stroke which can be counted upon to hit the ball truly, the only thing he should worry about is, as Alec Smith would say, "To knock the ball into the hole."

•

Nearly all good putters like to let the ball die into the hole.

So swing, swing, swing if you want to play better golf! Fight down any tautness wherever it may make its appearance. Strive for relaxed muscles throughout and encourage a feeling of laziness in the backswing and then start downward. Go back far enough, trust your swing, and then —swing the club head through.

•

Any man would be grateful, I believe, for any hints which would help him to get through this "tuning up" period with as little suffering as possible.

•

The second failing in part results from the first, although it is attributable also to the fact that the winter layoff impairs the player's sense.

•

For length and roll, hit drives slightly upward, and for accuracy and quick stopping, strike the irons and pitches slightly downward.

It is hard to make a beginner understand that the best way to get a brassie shot up from a close or cuppy lie is to "go down after it." The downward blow produces backspin and this spin forces the ball up.

•

Many bad shots are caused by a right elbow which soars away from the side of the body as the club is being taken back.

•

There is still another aid to be obtained from this proximity of the feet. It makes the turn of the left hip a simpler, easier matter and this also applies to the transference of weight where there is less distance to be covered. A player gets a world of leverage from this turn of the left hip.

•

I think there can be no question that the golf stroke ought to be dominated from first to last by the left arm.

The first failure is in the length of the backswing.

•

It makes little difference how long the head is kept down so long as one makes certain that the ball has actually been struck before the eye leaves it.

•

I don't try to putt with my body, but I never try to keep my body still. I'd like it to be free so it can move if the stroke demands it. The whole idea it seems to me is to do the thing in the simplest and most natural way.

•

I believe every teacher will advise that the putter-head should finish low. Obviously, unless it stops at impact, it cannot finish low unless something is done to flatten the arc of the follow-through. And that can be accomplished only by allowing the left wrist and arm to move in a forward line as the ball is struck.

The art of judging slope and speed is not entirely god-given.

•

As a rule, I prefer to putt with a little "borrow" to one with a perfectly straight line and I like to borrow from the left.

•

Almost all beginners are slicers and nearly all slicers strike downward. Very few players who hook habitually hit down.

•

Absolute concentration upon the ball is materially aided by substituting for the objective of the putt, instead of the hole itself, a spot on the green somewhere along the intended line. ... It should then be the player's aim to strike the ball so that it will roll directly over this spot, and he should forget the hole entirely except insofar as his mental picture of the length of the putt will affect the strength of his blow.

An examination of the grip used by expert golfers will show that in every instance the left hand is to some degree on top of the shaft.

•

A good part of the game is played between the ears; meaning that judgment, based on thought and experiences, is often as important as mechanical skill.

•

Rhythm and timing are the two things which we all must have, yet no one knows how to teach either.

•

The matter of bringing the feet closer together than most golfers has two distinct values. In the first place it reduces tension throughout the body. It is more natural to stand with the feet fairly close than it is to spread them out in the braced attitude so many golfers use.

Those who say dogmatically that to keep the left arm straight is correct, and to bend it is wrong, overlook the fact that the golf stroke consists of considerably more than one motion.

•

With the medium irons and short irons, the trouble that I have most often is failing to cock my wrists at the top. I am inclined sometimes to hang on to the club a little bit too tightly so that I don't get that nice rhythm.

Psychology of Golf

Courageous timidity, a most happy phrase, for it expresses exactly the qualities which a golfer, expert or not, must have in order to get the most from whatever mechanical ability he may have. Courageous, to keep trying in the face of ill luck or disappointment; and timidity, to appreciate and appraise the dangers to take chances beyond reasonable hope of success.

(Jones quoting J. H. Taylor)

•

Only a really good course will afford opportunity to use every club in the bag.

•

Golf is played more between the ears than on the golf course. This does not mean that anything like a superior mentality is required; but it does mean that there must be no mental daisy-picking while a shot is being played.

•

Championships are won on toast and tea, not on milk and honey.

Golf is said to be an humbling game, but it is surprising how many people are either not aware of their weaknesses or else reckless of consequences.

•

In match play, you have a single human opponent who may make some mistakes, but in stroke play, you are up against Old Man Par who never gets down in one putt and never takes three.

•

Golf may be...a sophisticated game. At least, it is usually played with the outward appearance of great dignity. It is, nevertheless, a game of considerable passion, either of the explosive type, or that which burns inwardly and sears the soul.

•

Don't hit the ball until you are ready, until every other consideration has been excluded from the mind.

If you play Old Man Par close, he will generally look out for the other fellow.

•

It is difficult to pick out one shot or to name one kind of situation which causes the most mental anguish. If I had to name one, I should say that a championship competitor would be more likely to pick up gray hairs in a bunker than anywhere else on the golf course.

•

Some emotions could not be endured with a golf club in my hands.

•

Golf is the only game that I know of that actually becomes harder the longer you play it.

•

Golf is also a game of temperament and, for some of us, even of temper.

Harry Vardon always said, "No matter what happens, keep on hitting the ball."

•

The more one plays competitive golf and the greater one's experience becomes, the more difficult it is to maintain unbroken concentration in a close match.

•

No virtue in this world is so oft rewarded as perseverance. Don't give up just because you are bunkered in three, and your opponent is on the green in two. You might hole out, and he might take three putts.

•

There are two kinds of golf—golf and tournament golf. In tournament golf, there's nothing that can put back what it takes out of you—the suffering, the worry over your game, the eternal grind of practice with thousands of spectators crowding in on you, the mental strain of a week's competition.

The most dangerous time when the cords of concentration are most apt to snap is when everything is going smoothly.

•

It is well to be apprised of all dangers, and the chances of failure, and the penalty likely to be incurred in the event of such failure ought to be weighed carefully before deciding upon the shot. But after taking the stance, it is too late to worry. The only thing to do then is to hit the ball!

•

Competitive golf, especially stroke play, demands that the player be continually on the lookout against himself.

•

I do not believe there is another sport that requires the uninterrupted, intense concentration of the mind than is demanded of a golfer in competition with others of anything like equal skill.

The main difficulty offered by a strong breeze arises from its effect upon the mind of the player.

•

Most failures from bunkers or rough results from topping, and this is so because tension has upset the stroke.

•

I have never attached much importance to the 'master eye' theory. I don't think it makes any difference which of a man's eyes is the stronger or whether he gazes at any particular point on the cover of the ball. All that he needs is to be able to measure the distance and to locate accurately the ball's position. I am told that he can do this better with two eyes than with one. I don't look at the ball with either my left eye or my right eye. I don't stare at any particular spot on it. I'm merely conscious of its location. I think that the position of my head [cocking to one side] is more important than any consideration of the left eye, because if you'll notice my swing when I hit the ball, my head is back.

Golf is a game of psychology. It is played in the six-inch course between the ears.

•

Of all the terrible things a man may do to a golf ball, the most demoralizing and the most mystifying is to "shank" it - which is hitting the ball with the socket of the clubface instead of the face itself.

•

In golf, we can never tell when the tables of fate will turn. The holing of one long putt may set us off on an inspired burst which will sweep us off our feet. So we can never be sure of victory or defeat until the last putt is in the hole. Until then we must play every shot as well as we possibly can. Having done that, we can do no more though the heavens fall.

•

A player certainly tries more quickly when playing before a large crowd.

Although some experience is required to avoid being frightened or annoyed by a large gallery, I think certainly that when this experience has been gained, to be followed about the course by a large number of spectators is a distinct advantage to a competitor.

•

I do not like making the pace. It gets harder and harder as you go. The other fellows, with nothing on their minds but their hair, are shooting the works while you keep wondering if you hadn't better be careful and try not to lose any strokes, which is the best possible way of losing them.

•

We hear "slow back" on every side, but "slow back" is not enough. There are numbers of players who are able to restrain their impulses to this extent, but who, once back, literally pounce upon the ball with uncontrolled fury. It is the leisurely start downward which provides for a gradual increase of speed without disturbing the balance and timing of the swing.

Confidence in the club, or the swing, or the shot, aids concentration because it banishes tension and strain; confidence in the result of a match or tournament makes impossible the concentration and hard work required to win.

•

Mental tension, that is keenness, never does any harm when it is accompanied by physical relaxation.

•

The thing to be careful of in the wind is to see that you don't let it rattle you. It baits you into pressing. When you're driving against a stiff breeze, you should take things a bit more easily than usual. Don't try to overcome the wind, but just accept your loss of distance and hit the ball comfortably down the fairway.

•

Too much ambition is a bad thing to have in a bunker.

It's quite a lot more comfortable to be a stroke or
two back of the pacemaker than up there setting
the pace yourself.

•

The average player ought to realize that he must
study his faults and learn to correct them in the
course of a round.

Philosophy of Golf

Golf has been called "the most human of games" and a "reflection of life." One reason that we enjoy it and that it challenges us is that it enables us to run the entire gamut of human emotions, not only in a brief space of time, but likewise without measurable damage either to ourselves or to others.

•

On why he didn't like to be called Bobby: "I think that when a man gets to be 58 years old, he ought to have outgrown a diminutive."

•

First come my wife and my children. Next comes my profession—the law. Finally, and never a life in itself, comes golf.

•

Golf is the closest game to the game we call life. You get bad breaks from good shots; you get good breaks from bad shots—but you have to play the ball where it lies.

Friends are a man's priceless treasures and a life rich in friendship is full indeed.

•

A strong back and a weak mind and a lot of this stuff they call the will to win, have made many a golfing champion who hadn't the shots or the heart or the character of some I could name.

•

You can only eat 2 eggs a day, wear 1 suit. All you need is enough money to stay even and be decent to your friends.

•

When praised for his honesty ..... "You may just as well praise me for not breaking into banks. There is only one way to play this game."

•

I do not have anything against the human race as a tribe, but I prefer them in small doses.

On the golf course, a man may be the dogged victim of inexorable fate, be struck down by an appalling stroke of tragedy, become the hero of unbelievable melodrama, or the clown in a side-splitting comedy—any of these within a few hours, and all without having to bury a corpse or repair a tangled personality.

•

The breaks will even themselves up in the long run - if the run is long enough.

•

I do not like an ill-natured loser. No one does. But I object equally to a winner or loser who makes light of the contest. Whether he has won or whether he has lost, a man owes it to his opponent to make him feel that the match has been a serious one.

•

No man learns to design a golf course simply by playing golf, no matter how well.

It always seemed and it seems today such an utterly useless and idiotic thing to stand up to a perfectly single shot, one that I know I can make a hundred times running without a miss—and then mess it up the one time I want to make it.

•

If fame can be said to attach to one because of his proficiency in the inconsequential performance of striking a golf ball, what measure of it I have enjoyed has been due in large part to Keeler and his gifted typewriter.

•

No matter how pretty you play your shots, no matter how well you swing or how sweetly the ball behaves—after all, it's only the championship that counts.

•

A golf tournament is all in the book before the first ball is driven.

Whatever may be a player's skill, he must have luck to win a championship of any kind, at least he must have no bad luck; golf is still a game rather than a science, and a game it is likely to remain. Possibly the feature of uncertainty is the chief reason for its popularity among players and spectators alike.

•

There is something wrong with a golf course which will not yield a score in the 60s to a player who has played well enough to deserve it...We are willing to have low scores made during the tournament and it is not our intention to rig the golf course so as to make it tricky.

•

A lot of the things you do wrong on a golf course, you do wrong because you're thinking too much about your swing. When you get on a golf course, you shouldn't think of anything but what happens from here to there. Just say, "Here's the ball, and I want to knock it over there,' and then go ahead and knock it over there."

The faculty, which the first-class player possesses, of quickly sizing up the requirements of a shot on a strange course, choosing the club, and the method of playing it, is what I mean by resourcefulness and judgment.

•

The golfer who is devoid of imagination of any kind will certainly never rise far above mediocrity.

•

I believe with modern equipment and modern players, we cannot make a good course more difficult or more testing for the expert simply by adding length...The only way to stir them up is by the introduction of subtleties around the greens.

•

In tournament play, especially in medal competition, it is the duty of every competitor to call attention to infractions of the rules and to see that the proper penalty is imposed.

There seems to be little appreciation today that golf is an amateur game, developed and supported by those who love to play it. Amateurs have built the great golf courses where the playing pros play for so much money; amateurs maintain the clubs and public links organizations that provide jobs for the working pros; amateurs spend millions of dollars each year on golf equipment and clothing; and amateurs rule and administer the game on both sides of the Atlantic. In this way, golf has prospered for several centuries. It would appear to be the best possible arrangement.

•

The men who are capable of complete concentration throughout an eighteen hole round can be counted upon the fingers of one hand.

•

The reward goes to him who plods along unruffled and unexcited, refusing to become angry with himself or the results of his efforts.

A player should form a habit of playing promptly, eliminating all wasted energy and unnecessary strain. There is always more ease, grace, and rhythm in the swing that begins with one or two leisurely regulated waggles, and proceeds without hurry and without hesitation.

•

But I must say here to every man who has beaten me in the past, and to every one who will beat me in the future, that their victories have not or will not come from want of effort on my part. If I find that I cannot concentrate on the game and work my hardest to win, I shall join the gallery and cheer for the men who have a better right than I to their place in the field.

Humor of Golf

One has never learned to master the game until he realizes that his best stroke is a mere accident and his worst stroke is good exercise.

(Jones quoting Eugene Black)

•

I once told a friend that the easiest way to determine the distance to the hole was by considering the size of people around the green. His reply was that there never were any people around the green when he was playing.

•

I remember that I was a very young man when I first played East Lake, my home course, in 63. Afterward, I confided to my father that I had mastered the secret of the game and that I should never go above 70 again. Next day I had to work my head off to get around in 77.

•

If you enter a tournament, and don't cheat, and happen to make the lowest score, they have to give you the cup.

I love to play, I love fishing and hunting and trap shooting and ping pong and chess and pool and billiards. At times, I love golf when I can get the shots going somewhere near right. It seems, in fact, that I love almost any pursuit except work.

•

Please don't think me unappreciative of my good fortune in the matter of championships. But there was so much luck in my winning that I feel more and more that the popular value of championship is a fictitious rating.

•

Funny how smartly you can boot away a big lead in a golf championship!

•

The difference between a sand trap and water hazard is the difference between a car crash and an airplane crash. You have a chance of recovering from a car crash.

You know, golf is a funny game. There never was a round of golf played in a big championship or just among friends, by experts or duffers, that didn't develop its humorous situations, and often really dramatic interludes.

•

...a strenuous reducing program immediately before an important championship would be a very dangerous thing. It is usually helpful to be keyed up, as the expression is, when one walks upon the first tee, but to be on such a physical "edge" that the nerves will be in a turmoil day and night is bound to be harmful.

•

I think a careless shot invariably costs more than a bad shot painstakingly played for it leaves the morale in a state of disorder.

•

I haven't played golf in eight years. But then, I haven't missed a putt in eight years, either.

...**golf is a funny game.** It is also a tantalizing, frustrating, fascinating game. Tournament golf can be heroic or tragic, a play of forces in which players and spectators alike may experience drama equal to that on any stage. And in any kind of golf, pathetic and ludicrous situations may succeed one another with kaleidoscopic rapidity.

•

The average golfer is not interested in winning championships. The chief benefits of the game for him must be recreation and the companionship of congenial friends. But I've always thought that if the game was worth playing at all, it was worth making some effort to play correctly.

•

My best scores have always been made when I have run into a streak in the midst of a round—late enough to permit me to get back to the clubhouse before I entirely regained consciousness.

The moment the average golfer attempts to play from long grass or a bunker or from a difficult lie of any kind, he becomes a digger instead of a swinger.

•

If your nose is close to the grindstone rough and you hold it down there long enough, soon you'll say there's no such thing as brooks that babble and birds that sing. These three will all your world compose: Just you, the stone and your goddammed nose.

•

There's a grand old girl up in Barbourville, Kentucky—Miss Nola Minton, who used to have a lot of wonderful show horses. She made hickory golf club shafts in the old days. Well, a few years ago she saw me with two bamboo canes and, not long after, she shipped me these hickory canes; and she wrote me a little note, 'You've been leaning on hickory all your life. It's too late to change now.'

Reflections on Golf

There was good reason to expect that improvement in manufacture and the introduction of new methods and materials might make even our long courses look silly and make jokes of our championships. It was not practical to think of buying more and more expensive ground to keep increasing the length of holes to make them fit for championship play as the ball became more and more powerful, particularly when this increase in power carried no actual advantage to the game in any conceivable form.

•

I could take out of my life everything except my experiences at St. Andrews and I'd still have a rich and full life.

•

The best competitive golfers are, I think, the distrustful and timorous kind who are always expecting something terrible to happen—pessimistic fellows who are always quite certain when they come upon the green that the ball furthest from the hole is theirs.

Every golfer worthy of the name should have some acquaintance with the principles of golf course design, not only for the betterment of the game, but for his own selfish enjoyment. Let him know a good hole from a bad one and the reasons for a bunker here and another there, and he will be a long way towards pulling his score down to respectable limits. When he has taught himself to study a hole from the point of view of the man who laid it out, he will be much more likely to play it correctly.

•

Amateurism, in my opinion, is entirely a matter of convenience, depending upon the financial condition of the individual. It is nice for a man to make a hobby of his favorite sport, to play it or leave it alone as he likes. But...it is fine to be an amateur if one can afford it.

•

Golf is like eating peanuts. You can play too much or too little. I've become reconciled to the fact that I'll never play as well as I used to.

I am not one who believes my era was the greatest necessarily because I lived in it. People today run faster, jump higher, and run farther and it's only material that they can play golf better. Ben Hogan has pretty well proved that they can. But the thing that makes a champion is not necessarily previous play. The man who works the hardest wins championships. Ben, with the game he has, will keep winning championships as long as he wants to badly enough.

•

The Grand Slam seemed to leave nothing lacking. By keeping on I might add one or more championships to the total, but it seemed that even the most I could hope for would be an anticlimax. I knew I could never do another Grand Slam, nor would I even try.

•

I discovered long ago that I had to control my temper in tournament play as a matter of utility, aside from considerations of decent behavior.

We can move all of our tees forward, if we wish, without investing more money in costly land, but we cannot keep on moving them backward.

•

I was not much of a practice-tee fellow. That was no good for me, because on the golf course you've got to make the first shot, not the eighth one. On a practice tee you haven't got that sense of responsibility.

•

I think I enjoyed playing in tournaments more before I began winning them, because then you've got nothing on your mind but your hat, and no special reputation to live up to, and no responsibilities.

•

I am not a believer in very heavy clubs. But there is no doubt that a heavier club tends to slow up one's swing to an extent which is sometimes very helpful.

Of all the courses I've played tournaments on, if I had to be sentenced to play only one course the rest of my life, I would pick St. Andrews in Scotland, because it changes so much, and there's nothing about it that's obvious.

•

American architecture allows practically no option as to where the drive shall go.

•

Now, let me ask what manner of golfer will be developed by courses of this nature? The answer is—a mechanical shot producer with little initiative and less judgment, and ability only to play the shot as prescribed.

•

The indifferent player should be allowed enough rope to hang himself and the punishment for a bad shot should not be an immediate one but should be postponed so that the player is in a bad strategic position for attacking the green.

In my humble opinion, St. Andrews is the most fascinating golf course I have ever played.

•

Medal competition is the most diabolical sort of golf because it puts so many worries into the player's head.

•

I used to think that if I could suppress a feeling of nervousness when starting out to play a match, I could then play a better and more thoughtful game. I have since come to think that the man who goes placidly on his way is often the easiest fellow to beat, for it is only the high-strung temperament that rises above its own ability to meet a great occasion.

•

In the final analysis there is little room for entertaining the hope that putting may be reduced to a science. Good putting is at best a fleeting blessing. Here today, gone tomorrow.

By 1975, someone will come along who they'll be comparing with Hogan, just as Hogan came along after me.

•

Sam Snead said to me one night at a Masters Club dinner, "Bob, tell me, which one of the championships that you won did you want to win the most?" I said, "Sam, it was always the one I was playing in at the time."

•

I have tried it both ways—setting the pace and trying to come up from behind. And I don't know which is harder. But either is harder for me than match play though I have been rather more successful at medal play.

•

Competitive golf is a curious thing. The best tournaments I have played have followed poor practice rounds and then a gradual turn for the better.

You never know who your friends are until you lose.

•

Quite honestly, I have no longing for the "old cheers, loud and free." I had my day long ago and I am quite content now to applaud with the other spectators. But the wonderful thing about golf is that it holds forever the interest of all who play it; and so I find myself today a member of a sort of fraternity of those who walk the fairways with me, with numbers considerably augmented by the many who have come since...The championships have been very much worth the effort they cost, but more important by far have been the expanding interests they brought and the avenues to friendships with individuals and groups of people they opened for me. That these rewards should endure so long makes it easy to see why for me golf will always be the greatest game.

•

What I particularly commend in a golfer is the patient waiting for opportunities.

In America we force the pitching shot and a player must have the full range of pitching clubs; while in Britain one rarely has to pitch if he prefers another shot.

•

In every club there is always at least one man who has the reputation of "making a poor game go a long way," the man who seems always to beat a player a bit better than himself. He doesn't do it by any divine inspiration, nor yet by any trick of fate. He simply uses his head, analyzing each situation as it confronts him, always keeping in view of his own limitations and powers. That is what we call judgment, and it is a lot easier to use good judgment than it is to learn to swing a club like Harry Vardon.

•

Sometimes when confidence has been shaken, it helps to use a new putter for a round or two until a few putts begin to drop and the player's morale has improved. But in the long run, the old horse is best.

There is no possibility of exaggerating the value of being able to hole all the short or missable putts.

·

Long waits at the tee constitute one of the severest problems of competitive golf. They break your concentration; throw you off stride.

·

Doesn't it show us all that we are silly little boys or fatuous asses to think that we can play golf without making a lot of bad shots.

·

I want especially to avoid comparisons or disparagements, either expressed or implied, of other golfers, professional or amateur. I especially do not like the phrase occurring more than once, "beating the pros at their own game." Actually, we were all playing the same game, and if I played less than they did, that should have been the concern of no one but me; presumably, I could have played more had I wanted to.

Every successful competitive golfer has learned to adopt a certain humility toward an opponent or an open championship field.

•

I am no lover of the habit of giving names to holes, but the trees and shrubs which give identity to the holes at Augusta are real enough: flowering peach, magnolia—the drive is alive with them, too; yellow jasmine, Carolina cherry, camellia—never was the iron gauntlet of challenge more skillfully concealed in velvet.

•

I think we must agree that all a man can do is beat the people who are around at the same time he is. He cannot win from those who came before any more than he can from those who may come afterward. It is grossly unfair to anyone who takes pride in the record he is able to compile that he must see it compared to those of other players who have been competing against entirely different people under wholly different conditions.

Acknowledgments

Grateful appreciation is extended to Jonesheirs, Inc., Martin B. Elgison, and the family of Bob Jones for permission to reprint certain short excerpts from *Golf Is My Game*, *Bobby Jones on Golf*, and the foreword to *The World of Golf* (Charles Price, Editor) in this work.

Thanks is also extended to world renowned artist Ed Lloyd for the drawings of Bob Jones he has generously created and which are displayed on these pages.

Additional gratitude is extended to my loyal staff, Gwynne Chason and Cindy Thompson, for their kind assistance in the preparation of the manuscript.

Another indispensable significant contribution is gratefully acknowledged from my dear friend, colleague and golfing partner (who owes me two strokes a side in our matches at East Lake, in the tradition of Watts Gunn), Dr. Robert Tyre Jones, IV, who has generously contributed the foreword.